Dear Elba, [illegible]

I'M
SERIOUSLY
JOKING

It was SERIOUSLY awesome
to meet you all!

Tom E. Moffatt

Published in 2021 by Write Laugh Books
Rotorua, New Zealand

Text © Tom E. Moffatt, 2021

Illustrations © Paul Beavis, 2021

www.tomemoffatt.com

ISBN 978-0-9951210-8-9 (print)
ISBN 978-0-9951210-9-6 (ebook)

A catalogue record for this book is available from the
National Library of New Zealand.

Cover design and illustrations: Paul Beavis
Developmental and copy editing: Anna Bowles
Proofreading: Vicki Arnott, Story Polisher
Print book and ebook design: Write Laugh Books

I'M SERIOUSLY JOKING

*

TOM E. MOFFATT

*

ILLUSTRATED BY PAUL BEAVIS

For Paul Beavis,

my seriously brilliant illustrator.

CONTENTS

TIME TO GET SERIOUS

I had loads of fun writing I'm Joking, my first collection of jokes. But I knew if I wanted to come up with another five hundred original jokes, I needed to get serious. So, I laid down some rules:

No watching TV.

No reading books.

No listening to podcasts.

… UNTIL I had written five jokes that day.

There were a few long nights and entertainment-free weeks, but more than enough fun and l a u g h - o u t - l o u d moments to keep me going. And in less than six months… I'm Seriously Joking was complete.

My goal was to provide tons of new jokes that you (and your friends and family) have never heard before. So, if I wrote a joke that seemed too obvious or familiar, I chucked it out and started over, resulting in five hundred completely fresh jokes.

I seriously hope you enjoy them!

Tom E. Moffatt

FAIRY-TALE JOKES

Once upon a time, I thought it would be a good idea to write a few jokes for my website. I've now written more than a thousand of them, and *The End* is nowhere in sight. In fact, joke-writing has become one of the most enjoyable chapters in my author story ... one that leads me in directions that I never imagined I would go. Like these fairy-tale jokes, for example.

I'M SERIOUSLY JOKING

Why does Goldilocks go round in circles?

She always goes just right

What did the emperor wear to his party?

His birthday suit

How do we know that fairy tales are made up?

Fairies don't have tails

What made the pile of mattresses wet?

The princess and the pee

How did Jack's mum find out about the giants?

Jack spilt the beans

FAIRY-TALE JOKES

 What stories do puppies like?

Furry tails

Why did Snow White win referee of the year?

She was the fairest of them all

When does Rumpelstiltskin put on weight?

When he wears a name badge

FAIRY-TALE JOKES

What did the witch in Hansel and Gretel say when she got back to her house?

Home, sweet home

Why did Prince Charming and Rapunzel grow their hair long?

So they could live hippily ever after

What did the wolf say to his toast?

All the butter to eat you with

 Which prince gets left behind in the forest?

Foot prints

What do you call a princess with a numb bum?

Sleeping booty

I'M SERIOUSLY JOKING

What does Cinderella eat for a midnight feast?

Pumpkin pie

Why did Jack call the police?

He'd been stalked

What do you get if you walk far, far away?

Pus in boots

STUDENT ONE: Who ate the Gingerbread man?

STUDENT TWO: It wasn't me, dude

What did Hansel say when he lost his way?

Oh, crumbs!

FAIRY-TALE JOKES

Why do you need a tape measure in the shoemaker's shop?

It's elf service

What weighs four tons and wears glass slippers?

Cinderelephant

SCHOOL-TIME SHENANIGANS

I've spent lots of time in schools. Obviously, I had to go to one when I was a child, like it or not. But as an adult I became a teacher and taught in schools all over the world for over ten years. Nowadays, I get to visit schools as an author, which is much more fun. All I have to do is tell jokes and stories. And it's no coincidence that many of these jokes and stories are set in schools.

I'M SERIOUSLY JOKING

Why don't pencils need legs?

They are stationary

 ### *What's less than a metre long but packed full of kids?*

A school yard

How does a light bulb learn?

With flash cards

Why did the detective spend all day in the classroom?

She was looking into a pencil case

SCHOOL-TIME SHENANIGANS

Why did the roofer's daughter love school?

She was always top of the class

Why did the girl carry a branch to school?

It was her reading log

What happened to the teacher when his arms, legs and body fell off?

He became the head of the school

SCHOOL-TIME SHENANIGANS

Why did the boy have bits of metal in his teeth?

It was his staple diet

How does Maths affect your language skills?

It gives you word problems

Why does school keep you fit?

You do lots of exercises

What do you call a pencil that doesn't write?

Pointless

How do you make consonant blends?

With a word processor

I'M SERIOUSLY JOKING

Why did the boy throw a brick through a classroom window?

It was break time

What did the balloon hate about school?

Pop quizzes

Why did the school children fight, steal and lie?

They didn't have any principals

How do you break bad behaviour?

In d'tension

Why did the bully cross the road?

He was chicken

Why do snowmen never learn anything?

They are too cool for school

What does fun do at school?

Lessens

FAST ONES

Here's a collection of fast-paced jokes that are all related to transport. Many of my jokes are actually concocted at top speed, because I often think them up while I'm driving.

I'M SERIOUSLY JOKING

What breaks every time you use it?

A car

Why did the detective think the mechanic did it?

He had an auto motive

What do you call a go-kart with no wheels?

A stop-kart

BOY: *I can ride on one wheel!*

DAD: Wheely?

FAST ONES

What do you call a car that runs on vegetable broth?

A stock car

★ **WOMAN:** *I keep getting attacked by my own bike.* ★

THERAPIST: That sounds like a vicious cycle.

What has four wheels and is made of cardboard?

A box car

What do you call a pencil with wheels?

A stationery vehicle

I'M SERIOUSLY JOKING

What do you call a car you're not allowed to drive?

A carn't

 ### Why did the man kick his car?

It needed toeing

What's another name for paper planes?

Aircraft

How do baby sheep get to hospital?

In a lambulance

FAST ONES

What do racing drivers drink before Formula One?

Breast milk

When does a bus get wet?

When it's dew

 ## Why did the girl bring her boat to a party?

It was an icebreaker

What's another word for a dental boat?

A tooth ferry

Who's in charge of all the other vehicles?

The coach

What's the similarity between a car and a baby's bottom?

They both have wipers

Why did the motorbike fall over?

It was two-tyred

What goes choo-choo on the end of a pencil?

A train of thought

FAST ONES

TOILET HUMOUR

The most popular collection on my website is my bum jokes. It gets thousands of hits every month, and if you type *bum* (or *butt*) *jokes* into Google, I'm usually the top result. For this reason, I thought it would be a good idea to include a bit more toilet humour in this book.

I'M SERIOUSLY JOKING

What's a bum's favourite day?

A bidet

When does a businessman feel pooped?

When he's bogged down with work

How do you make coffee in a toilet?

With a plunger

Why shouldn't you play Minecraft on the toilet?

It might get blocked

What do you say to a photo-bombing toilet?

Urinal the photos

TOILET HUMOUR

How do you get your arm down a toilet?

U-bend it

What did the poo say when it was flushed down the toilet?

Weeeeeee!

When did the baby poo want to swim in the toilet?

When it could touch the bottom

What did the constipated witch say?

Hubble bubble toilet trouble

TOILET HUMOUR

How do we know Elvis was still King when he died?

He was on the throne

Why was the old toilet always flushed?

Everyone kept yanking his chain

 What happens if you get stuck on an aeroplane toilet?

Your cheeks get flushed

When does toilet paper keep on wiping?

When it's on a roll

I'M SERIOUSLY JOKING

Why did the girl have crappy hair?

She used a toilet brush

Which lizard lives down the toilet?

A commode dragon

What's better than an in-house joke?

An out-house joke

How do you upload to a toilet?

By logging in

What happened to the toddler who drank a whole bottle of Coke?

She went potty!

TOILET HUMOUR

Why did the toilet throw a party?

It got engaged

Where do poos go to sleep?

In a bedpan

DINOSAUR ROMP

Some collections are
harder to write than others.
This was one of the difficult ones,
probably because dinosaur jokes
have been roaming the playground
for millions of years, which makes
it hard to find original ones
amongst the old fossils.

I'M SERIOUSLY JOKING

Why didn't dinosaurs tell jokes?

They were prehysterical

What do you call a clueless dinosaur?

A dunnosaur

Which dinosaur can't sit down?

A mega-sore-arse

What do you call a dinosaur with its head in the sand?

Fossil-eyes

Why did the dinosaurs only want twenty-five letters in the alphabet?

Their X stinked

DINOSAUR ROMP

 I've brought you a small female dinosaur!

Rapter?

No, I just left her in the cage

Which dinosaur gets you in trouble?

The teacher-saw-us

What did cavemen use to cut down trees?

A chainosaur

Why would dinosaurs eat motor vehicles?

They are car-nivores

DINOSAUR ROMP

What did the religious dinosaur say?

Let us prey

Which dinosaur always spills your cuppa?

Tea-wrecks

 What do you call a dinosaur that only ate French apples?

A pomme-nivore

How did dinosaurs serve cavemen?

On an armour plate

What do you call a short-sighted dinosaur?

A barely-saw-us

I'M SERIOUSLY JOKING

Which dinosaur comes from the Tree-assic period?

A Stickosaurus

What's another word for dinosaur?

Thesaurus

Did you hear about the skunkosaurus?

It stinked

What do you get if dinosaurs try to drive?

Rex

How did the pterodactyl feel when it flew into a cliff?

Pterrible

How does a Tyrannosaurus Rex order meat?

Raw!

DOCTOR, DOCTOR JOKES

At first, I found Doctor, Doctor jokes rather difficult to write. Then I realised that you need to approach them slightly differently. You have to think of the way that a doctor might respond, then you come up with a funny situation that might incite that response. Nowadays, they're one of my favourite kinds of jokes to play with.

I'M SERIOUSLY JOKING

Doctor, doctor, I just swallowed an eagle.

Well, that's going to make your throat soar.

 Doctor, doctor, I've just gone around the waiting room and taken everyone's temperature and blood pressure.

You're really testing my patients.

Doctor, doctor, everything I see is in black and white!

You do look like you've lost colour.

Doctor, doctor, it feels like the ceiling is slowly coming down on me.

You just need to lie low for a few days.

Doctor, doctor, I think I'm turning into a pirate!

Open wide and say 'Arrrrgh!'

Doctor, doctor, everything I sing is out of key.

That doesn't sound very good.

Doctor, doctor, it feels like a dark cloud has been following me around for weeks.

You do look a little under the weather.

DOCTOR, DOCTOR JOKES

Doctor, doctor, I can't stop stealing.

Take a seat and I'll call the police!

Doctor, doctor, I keep thinking I'm your bank account.

Okay, you've gained my interest.

 Doctor, doctor, I only seem to be able to turn left!

That's not right!

I'M SERIOUSLY JOKING

Doctor, doctor, I keep thinking I'm a toilet.

You do look a little flushed.

Doctor, doctor, I can't make any jokes and find nothing funny.

That sounds serious.

Doctor, doctor, I'm hearing an echo.

I'll be with you in a moment.
I'll be with you in a moment.

Doctor, doctor, I can't stop shaking this cream.

Well, it looks like you're getting butter.

DOCTOR, DOCTOR JOKES

Doctor, doctor, I feel like I'm under a microscope.

Let's take a closer look at you.

Doctor, doctor, every day I seem to double in size.

You need to see a shrink.

DOCTOR, DOCTOR JOKES

Doctor, doctor, everything I hold slips out of my grasp.

You just need to get a grip.

Doctor, doctor, my identical twin and I are overcome with worry!

You both look beside yourself.

Doctor, doctor, I feel like I'm made out of paper.

Yes, I can see you look tearable.

Doctor, doctor, I think I'm a library book.

Okay, I'm just going to check you out.

BIRD BANTER

When I first started
writing jokes, I was winging it.
I'd just think about each topic and
hope the jokes would come to me.
These days, after writing thousands of
jokes, I know my process pretty well. I
started this category by brainstorming
everything to do with birds. Then I googled a
list of different kinds of bird, followed by bird
vocabulary and idioms. I then took these
words and phrases, playing with them
one at a time until a joke came to
me. It wasn't too long before I'd
hit my target of twenty
bird jokes.

I'M SERIOUSLY JOKING

Which bird can't sing properly?

A hummingbird

When do birds eat a lot?

When they've got worms.

Why did the golfer get thrown off the course?

He kept shooting eagles

What should you say when you see a low-flying mallard?

Duck!

BIRD BANTER

What did the baby goose say on the first day of migration?

Are we there yet?

Where do birds drink milk?

In their nestlé

 Which bird flies closest to heaven?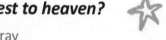

A bird of pray

How did the eagle get famous?

On a talon show

What do baby birds drink from?

A beaker

★ **Why do birds tweet?** ★

They don't like Facebook

BIRD BANTER

What do you call books about baby birds?

Chick lit

 ### Which bird is the least fit?

A puffin

What do birds do when they don't know the answer?

Wing it

When do you see a bird in a car?

When it's flipped

I'M SERIOUSLY JOKING

Why did the hunters have feathers in their stew?

They were having a lark

Why did the golfer keep a shotgun in his golf bag?

So he could shoot a birdie

What should you do if a bird gets stuck in your throat?

Swallow

Which bird flies itself into a cage?

A jailbird

BIRD BANTER

☆ *Why did the bird say 'Baaaa!'?* ☆

It got in with the wrong flock

What do you call a bird that always sits on your head?

A burden

WILD WIT

One of the mistakes I made when I first started writing jokes was that the categories I selected were too broad. I chose things like animals, food and sports. Sure, this made it easier for me at the time, but it wasn't sustainable. These days, I try to narrow my search by using more specific categories, such as wild animals and pets.

I'M SERIOUSLY JOKING

Why did the bear keep getting bigger?

It was an ex-panda

Where do wild animals get their exercise?

The jungle gym

What's baby Kangaroo's favourite book?

Where's Wallaby?

Why do leopards make terrible cat burglars?

They're always spotted

What eats you when you open it?

A pack of wolves

WILD WIT

When should you listen to a rhinoceros?

When it's in charge

Why do pandas prefer climbing to walking?

They have bear feet

 Did you hear a lion?

No, but I herd of elephants

I'M SERIOUSLY JOKING

What do you get if you cross a monkey with a flower?

A chimp-pansy

What does a frog say when it gets a hare in its throat?

Rabbit

WILD WIT

 Why do elephants have long trunks?

So they can pick their toes

What did the buffalo say when her eldest child left the herd?

Bison

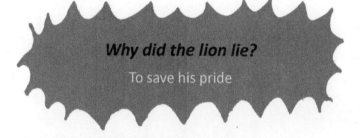

Why did the lion lie?

To save his pride

What's the least interesting wild animal?

A wild bore

☆ **Why did the lion carry a cell phone?** ☆

For the call of the wild

I'M SERIOUSLY JOKING

★ **What do you call a panda in a newspaper?** ★

A red panda

Where do chimpanzees hang out?

Monkey bars

Which animal wins the romp in the swamp comp?

The rhymenoceros

What key opens a banana?

A monkey

WILD WIT

How did the cat win the race?

It was a cheetah

LIMERICK LAUGHS

Okay, so limericks are not technically jokes. But they are funny, so I thought I'd include them. They're also great fun to write. You should give them a go...

I'M SERIOUSLY JOKING

There once was a young girl called Bess,
Whose clothes were a horrible mess,
They hung from her back,
Like a hessian sack,
But this young girl just couldn't care less.

There once was a young boy called Pete,
Who tried scoffing a pie with his feet,
He got sauce 'tween his toes,
The crust up his nose,
And he had very little to eat.

There once was a lady called Jenny,
Who bought a new car for a penny,
It was the greatest of deals,
Till she counted the wheels,
'Cos it turned out it didn't have any.

There once was a man from wherever,
Who used to wear nothing but leather,
When his undies went rotten,
He switched them for cotton,
And now he feels light as a feather.

LIMERICK LAUGHS

There once was a young boy called Mark,
Who wanted to glow in the dark,
He dressed up in nylon,
Climbed up a pylon,
And boy did that boy make a spark!

I'M SERIOUSLY JOKING

There once was a tiger called Tigger,
Who wanted his den to be bigger,
He tried using his jaws,
And retractable claws,
But eventually called in a digger.

There once was a young boy whose mother,
Decided he needed a brother,
She found a small goat,
Which she dressed in a coat,
To make those kids look like each other.

LIMERICK LAUGHS

There once was a girl from the Strand,
Who brought up a lion by hand,
As the lion got older,
It ate up to her shoulder,
Which wasn't quite what she had planned.

There once was a young boy whose habit,
Was to hop round the field like a rabbit,
In the blink of an eye,
He was put in a pie,
And that was the end of his habit.

There once was a girl from New York,
Who incessantly wanted to talk,
Her friends and her peers,
Stuck their thumbs in their ears,
Until somebody gave her a cork.

I'M SERIOUSLY JOKING

There once was a young man from Ealing,
Who had the most terrible feeling,
He drank water all day,
To take it away,
Till his vomit splashed over the ceiling.

There once was a foolish old bloke,
Who drank twenty litres of Coke,
That silly old chappy,
Was hyper and happy,
Till the dentist's bill left him quite broke.

There once was a young girl called Mary,
Who wanted to be a real fairy,
She made up a potion,
From shampoo and lotion,
But it just made her turn rather hairy.

There once was a runner called Rita,
Who was so fast that no one could beat her,
When they checked in her pocket,
They found a small rocket,
And realised that she was a cheater.

LIMERICK LAUGHS

There once was a trendy giraffe,
Who knitted a forty-foot scarf,
It wrapped round and round,
From his ears to the ground,
So tightly the poor creature barfed.

I'M SERIOUSLY JOKING

There once was a young boy called Mike,
Who rode three hundred miles on his bike,
Then as if in slow motion,
He crashed in the ocean,
Getting home was a bit of a hike.

There once was a teacher, Miss Whickers,
Who spent her days chomping on Snickers,
If you cut her supply,
In the blink of an eye,
She'd get a big knot in her knickers.

There once was an old man whose hair
Started to grow everywhere,
From the tops of his toes,
To right out of his nose,
So then he looked just like a bear.

There once were two little white mice,
Who were certain that cats could be nice,
They gave one some cheese,
Said thank you and please,
But weren't able to do such things twice.

There once was a knackered old chap,
Who lay down in the road for a nap,
He was certainly tyred,
The day he expired,
And he's now just a mark on a map.

FARTY FARCE

Here's another collection for the fans of my bum jokes. For those of you less inclined towards toilet humour... pardon me!

I'M SERIOUSLY JOKING

What's another word for old farts?

Has beans

Why do hippies ring when they fart?

Because of their bell-bottoms

What happens at the crack of Dawn?

She breaks wind

Why should you stop farting when you have diarrhoea?

You'll run out of wind

How did the lieutenant clear the room?

He pulled rank

FARTY FARCE

What makes the reaper so grim?

He always lets it RIP

I'M SERIOUSLY JOKING

How does a ninja fart?

Silent but deadly

LANDLORD: Why does my apartment stink so much?

TENANT: It's the flat-u-lent

FARTY FARCE

☆ **Why did the furniture removal man always eat beans?** ☆

So he could clear a room in seconds

What do you say when two bums get married?

Conflatulations

How do fighter pilots make a sonic boom?

By passing wind

Why should you never fart in a lift?

It's wrong on so many levels

What happened to the cheeky fart at school?

It got expelled

I'M SERIOUSLY JOKING

★ *How do you fart with love?* ★

From the bottom of your heart

What's the smelliest day of the year?

Farters' day

What did the bum sing when it was in the bath?

I'm forever blowing bubbles

Why did the butt join the school orchestra?

It was a wind instrument

 What made Einstein's hair stick up?

Brain farts

FARTY FARCE

What happened to the bum hat?

It blew off

What did Shakespeare say after he farted?

It is butt wind

DATE & TIME TRICKERY

Time flies, whether you're having fun or not. It doesn't seem all that long since I was that short, shy kid sitting in the corner reading one of the tall, skinny joke books that I got for Christmas every year. But nearly forty years have passed – most of which *were* fun – and I'm now writing joke books of my own that will hopefully find their way into the hands of many joke-lovers this Christmas.

I'M SERIOUSLY JOKING

Why did the stopwatch stop running?

It was pressed for time

What do you call a clock with no hour or minute hands?

A second-hand clock

When is being punctual dangerous?

When it's two sharp

Why did the time traveller disappear from his birthday party?

He didn't like the present

What's the tastiest day of the week?

Sundae

DATE & TIME TRICKERY

Why does time slow down after a meal?

It always goes back four seconds

Why's it a bad idea to live in a clock tower?

You're always behind the times

You said it was time for dinner, so I ate a clock!

What's the best day for decision-making?

Choose-day

DATE & TIME TRICKERY

Which day of the year is usually a disaster?

Mayday

What time does breakfast finish?

Ate o'clock

Why did the chef skip a key ingredient?

He was running out of thyme

What's it called when you can't get out of bed for a fortnight?

A too weak holiday

Why are most clocks big and round?

They always have seconds

I'M SERIOUSLY JOKING

Which fruit does time eat?

Dates

Why did the dad take his kids to a Rolex factory?

For some quality time

What did the pocket watch say to the grandfather clock?

I love you big time

Why did the window crack up?

It was break time

 When should boys wake up?

At son-rise

DATE & TIME TRICKERY

What time does ballet class begin?

At ten tutu

MUSIC MISCHIEF

People's
taste in music is
even more diverse than their
taste in jokes. When writing either, you
can't please everyone. Often, the jokes that I
think are really good won't get a laugh, yet
the ones that I wanted to scrap are a
major hit. So I aim to keep things as
varied as possible and try them out
on as many guinea pigs as I can.

I'M SERIOUSLY JOKING

 What do music teachers wear?

Chords

How did the microphone feel when it got plugged in?

Amped

Why did the man place his ear against a set of coloured pens?

He was listening to the blues

How does music keep you sane?

It gives you a sound mind

Why did the dollar bill join a choir?

It was a tenner

Which vegetable makes you dance?

Beets

 What do you call someone who composes music on a sewing machine?

A Singer songwriter

What happened to the rabbit drummer?

It got caught in a snare

What goes boing, boing, boing, boing, boing, booooiiiing, boing?

A rubber band

MUSIC MISCHIEF

Why did the rock star need a bucket?

To make musick

What do you call a high-pitched version of yourself?

Your alto ego

Why did the keyring get kicked out of the band?

It was off-key

What music does an atlas listen to?

Country

 What do you call a pod of whales singing together?

An orcastra

I'M SERIOUSLY JOKING

Who makes the most noise in church?

Hymn

What did the piece of golden foil do for a living?

It was a rapper

Why did the poo get kicked out of the choir?

It was always humming

What does a musician play when he has an overinflated ego?

Pop

MUSIC MISCHIEF

 If my bedroom was a symphony it would be called A Major Mess.

Why did the party boat sink?

Too much heavy metal

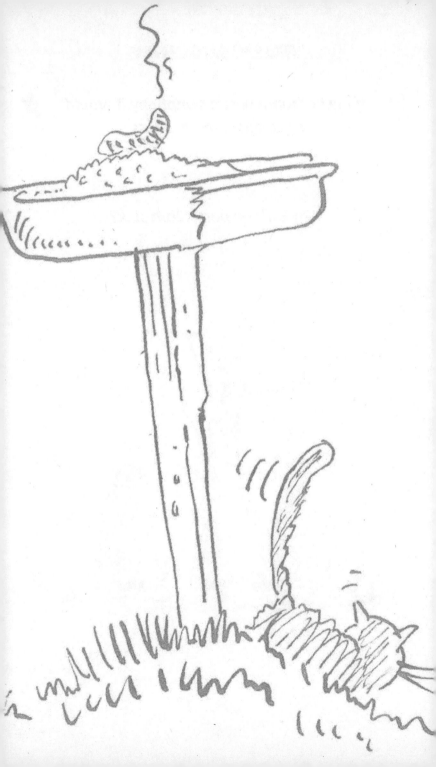

PET PLAYFULNESS

I wondered if pet jokes might
be too narrow a category, then I thought
about all the pets I've had over the years.
These include rabbits, dogs, cats, mice,
hamsters, fish, a tortoise, a slow worm,
a gecko and two iguanas, which left me
with quite a few options.

Why does an oyster make a terrible pet?

It's shelfish

*How do you make dog-flavoured
ice cream?*

Whippet

What's the best pet for beginners?

A guinea pig

PET PLAYFULNESS

When should you follow your dog?

When it takes the lead

Why was the robo-dog ignored by real dogs?

He didn't make scents

 Which pet can power a car?

Petrolium

I'M SERIOUSLY JOKING

How much do stray dogs weigh?

A pound

Why did the dog get married?

She needed a groom

PET PLAYFULNESS

 What does a tree use to scare off intruders?

Its bark

Why did the boy wear a dog's collar to school?

He wanted to be the teacher's pet

What's a zombie's favourite pet?

A rot-weiler

BOY IN A PET SHOP: What's the smallest pet you've got?

PET-SHOP OWNER: My newt

 Why are dog owners great at making ice creams?

They are good with a scoop

I'M SERIOUSLY JOKING

What's the most common household pet?

Fleas

What's the best pet to protect a tree house?

A budgerieguarddog

★ **How do you know when a gecko wants out of its vivarium?** ★

It starts climbing the walls

What do you call a dog that barks too much?

A husky

PET PLAYFULNESS

Why did the soldier buy some tropical fish?

He already had a tank

What did the wave say to the dog?

Fetch

Where do cats leave gifts for you?

In the litterbox

KEPT IN SUSPENSE

BY CLIFF HANGAR

FUNNY BOOK TITLES

I love coming up with the author names for funny book titles, but when naming children you need to make sure you don't inadvertently crack a joke. For example, if your surname is Moore, you probably shouldn't call your child Juno or Chase. I personally need to avoid names starting with the letter K, because K. Moffatt sounds like a bike accident.

I'M SERIOUSLY JOKING

Dropping Off
by Peter Doubt

Ready or Not, Here I Come
by Haiden Sikh

Door-to-Door Sales
by Belle Ringer

Healthy Snacks
by Ita Napple

FUNNY BOOK TITLES

Life on the Lake

by Rowan Boates

Yoga for Boys

by Ben D. Mann

Kept in Suspense

by Cliff Hangar

Here's an Example

by Caysen Pointe

 ### Dangerous Driving Conditions

by I. C. Rhodes

FUNNY BOOK TITLES

 Brilliant Acting

by Oscar Winner

Staying Happily Married

by B. Faithful

Love Songs

by Omar Darling

It's NOT an Orange

by Amanda Rin

Getting Lost

by Ron Waye

I'M SERIOUSLY JOKING

I Can't Stop Myself
by Anna Nutha

An Artist's Journey
by Drew Pictures

Collecting Honey
by B. Hives

How to Take a Joke
by Joss Kidding

Life's a Beach
by C. Shore

Gardening in Autumn

by Ray Cleaves

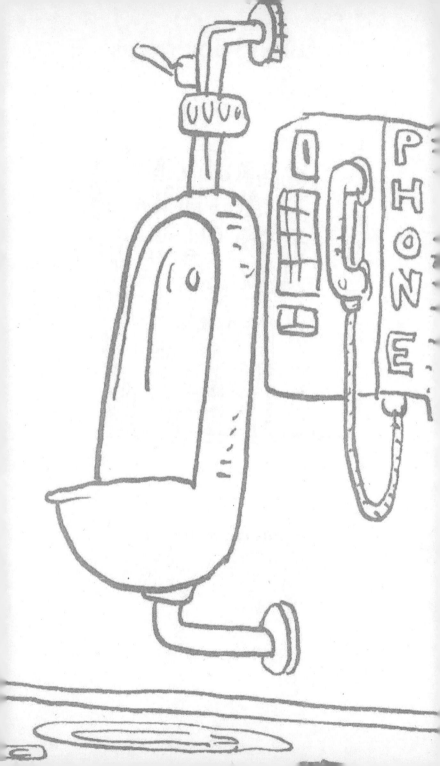

COMPUTER CAPERS

Sometimes, working with computers is not funny at all. Here are some computer-based jokes to think about the next time you feel like throwing one out of the window.

I'M SERIOUSLY JOKING

When do children have too much screen time?

When they're left to their own devices

Why shouldn't computers drive cars?

They often crash

How does a chicken control a computer?

With a double cluck

What made Eve's computer crash?

Too many bytes of the Apple

How do you track what's happening on the internet?

Keep tabs on it

How do you unlock Google?

With keywords

★ **Why did the lady take her laptop up a volcano?** ★

To find a hotspot

I'M SERIOUSLY JOKING

What do robots eat for dinner?

Microchips

I went into town on a computer disk. It was a hard drive.

What did the computer say after making a binary joke?

lol

Why couldn't the police find the computer hacker?

He'd gone phishing

COMPUTER CAPERS

Why did the boy saw a dollar into quarters?

He wanted some bitcoins

 ### What happened when I only ate apples for three days?

iPood

Why did the woman reverse all the way to the computer store?

She needed a backup drive

I'M SERIOUSLY JOKING

Why did the fisherman get hired by an IT firm?

He was a net-work specialist

How did the computer programmer spread his virus?

With a hacking cough

Which computers do they use at McDonalds?

Big Macs

Why did the girl drop her computer?

She wanted to make it 64 bits

Why did Elsa restart her computer?

It was frozen

COMPUTER CAPERS

What do you call a phone next to a urinal?

An IP phone

HOME HYSTERICS

The more jokes I write,
the harder it is to find suitable
categories. I've already done the
obvious ones, such as dogs, vegetables
and Halloween, so I now need to dig deeper.
This time, I thought I'd start a little closer to
home with things from around the house.

I'M SERIOUSLY JOKING

What did the lady say to the termites?

You've eaten me out of house and home

Why didn't the snail talk about its travels?

It was too close to home

What do you call a window that breaks easily?

A pain

Where do rulers live?

On the home straight

What happened when the boy put a booby trap under his mum's bed?

She hit the roof

HOME HYSTERICS

 Why couldn't the boat go home?

It had lost its quay

What happened to the firefighters who met on the job?

They got on like a house on fire

What happened when the knife and fork raced home?

It was a drawer

When is it a bad idea to sit on your deck?

When you live in a house of cards

HOME HYSTERICS

 Where do you get more stuff for your home?

The seller

Why was the windowpane sent to jail?

It was framed

Where can you find edible undies?

In a pant-tree

What should you do if your wardrobe door is open?

Closet

 Why should you never do business with an awning?

They're shady

I'M SERIOUSLY JOKING

Why did the retired farmer spend his days standing over an oven?

He was an ex-tractor fan

How do you get water out of a pipe?

Force it

Why did the man smash his kitchen benchtop with a sledgehammer?

It was a counter attack

Where's the best place to do CPR?

The living room

Why did the nail need pulling out?

It was in a jamb

HOME HYSTERICS

What does a house wear?

Address

WORLDLY WONDERS

When I was fifteen, I went
on a school exchange programme to
Zanzibar, Tanzania, for an entire month.
Naturally, it completely blew my mind, and
since then travelling has been one of my biggest
passions. I have lived in several different countries
and visited many others, but these days – with
three young kids – most of my travelling is done
via books and movies. These jokes of the
world gave me chance to escape my
writing desk for a short while.

I'M SERIOUSLY JOKING

How does the sun know when she's set behind the sea?

Her-eye's-in

What did the goose say to her husband as they migrated?

Uganda

Why do volcanoes erupt?

For the crater good

How does Mother Earth serve dinner?

On a tectonic plate

Why did the king turn all of his sand into glass?

So the coast was clear

What happened to the explorer who travelled in a teapot?

He went around the world in a tea daze

Where do zombies go on holiday?

The Dead Sea

Why couldn't the boat cross the Equator?

It had a terrible latitude

What happened when the explorer walked through a herb garden?

He crossed a thyme zone

WORLDLY WONDERS

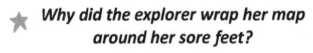 **Why did the explorer wrap her map around her sore feet?**

It was a relief map

Earth. It means the world to me.

Did you hear about the monster that ate an entire country?

It was Hungary

Why did the tectonic plate get blamed for the earthquake?

It was her fault

 Which flower helps you navigate the world?

A compass rose

I'M SERIOUSLY JOKING

Why do most human beings stay on Earth?

They like the atmosphere

What did the mountain climber feel when he achieved his goal?

Relief

Where should you go on holiday if you're feeling uptight?

Grease

Why did the sailor have wet socks when he wasn't at sea?

He was in continent

Why does Mother Earth keep spinning?

It's good for her core muscles

**Which country doesn't like
Thanksgiving?**

Turkey

TWIDDLY TONGUE TWISTERS

While they're
not technically
jokes, tongue twisters
are fun and can also be
quite funny, especially
when they're extremely
difficult. Try saying these
ones three times, as
quickly as you can.

I'M SERIOUSLY JOKING

Ten tenors' tonsils tingled to two tonsil-tingling tunes.

Billy barely bullied Barry but Barry battered Billy back.

These three fleas fought flies for fun.

Riley rides a wheely really wildly.

 Thor thought he saw four foes, though those foes thought they fought for Thor.

TWIDDLY TONGUE TWISTERS

Rose grows rows of roses,
Those roses grow in rows,
One row of roses grows and grows,
It grows higher than Rose's nose.

The little lolly-licker licked a lot of little lollies.

★ *Sue sees sushi so she shows Suzie* ★
some sushi.

TWIDDLY TONGUE TWISTERS

Eeny meeny miny moe,
Many moaning moaners moan.
What's mine is mine, so moan alone.
Eeny meeny moany moan.

Betty bought a better bit of butter, but
I'd better butter Betty's butter better.

 Murray Mary married Mary Murry,
making Mary Mary very merry.

Poopy Poppy pooped a pipe of
purple poopoo.

Feel free to suck four suckers, sir, for
four suckers are free for sucking.

I'M SERIOUSLY JOKING

Sarah saw several sorry sewers sewing serious saris.

One day Wendy wondered whether the weather would one day wither.

Baby Bobby bites Barbie's booby.

She's sure she saw a sea shore see-saw.

Cam can come to Kathmandu, but can Cam come to Cameroon too?

The hotshot shot a short, sharp shot to hit the chart's top spot.

TWIDDLY TONGUE TWISTERS

Our royal ruler rules really royally.

SIMPLE SIMON JOKES

We
can all be
a   bit   simple
at times. Here are
some Simple Simon and
Dense   Denise   jokes   that
reflect the inner idiot within us all.

I'M SERIOUSLY JOKING

Why did Dense Denise marry the football player?

She was told he was a keeper

Why did Simple Simon throw his alarm clock away?

It was going off

Why did Dense Denise take a ladder to an interview?

So she could get hired

What do you call an idiot with three packets of flour?

Romantic

SIMPLE SIMON JOKES

Why did Simple Simon join the orchestra?

So they could play the fool

Why did Dense Denise fill her suitcase with torches?

She was told to pack light

Why did Simple Simon put his phone in a field of bulls?

It needed charging

How many idiots does it take to change a light bulb?

I don't know

Really? I thought you'd know that one!

SIMPLE SIMON JOKES

Why did Simple Simon eat his test paper?

His teacher said it was a piece of cake

Why did Simple Simon cry after throwing his phone out the window?

He forgot to put it in flight mode

Why did Dense Denise bury a clock?

She wanted to grow some thyme

Why did Simple Simon buy a new pair of Levi's?

Someone told him he had bad genes

Why did Dense Denise run screaming from art class?

The teacher said they were going to dye

I'M SERIOUSLY JOKING

Why did Simple Simon kick the coffin?

It was supposed to be a wake

QUIZ MASTER: What's the capital of Canada?

DENSE DENISE: C

Why did Simple Simon take a glue gun to work?

He was told to stick to his day job

What do you call an idiot going backwards?

Toidi

Why did Dense Denise have a touchy stomach?

She swallowed the wrong kind of tablet

SIMPLE SIMON JOKES

★ *Why did Simple Simon sit down to chew gum?* ★

He didn't want to overachieve

Why did Simple Simon sweat while he painted his house?

He put on three coats

FARMYARD FUN

Writing jokes can feel a bit like farming. Each collection is its own field, and the seeds are all the related words and phrases that I can gather. Not all of them will grow into something harvestable, but those that show promise are fed and nurtured until I eventually have a crop of twenty usable jokes.

I'M SERIOUSLY JOKING

What do farmers do when there aren't enough hours in the day?

Harvest time

Which chore do chickens avoid?

Laying the table

What did the sheep say when it fell in love?

I only have eyes for ewe

How do farmers get into space?

With a tractor beam

What do you call a deer with pink contact lenses?

A colourful eye-dear

FARMYARD FUN

How do farmers like their hair cut?

In a crop

 What do you call a creature that's half
cow, half bull?

A breed of its own

I'M SERIOUSLY JOKING

What happened to the farmer who was caught stealing hay?

He didn't get bail

How did the farmer find his missing cow?

He tractor

★ **What did the farmer say when someone stole his cattle feed?** ★

Hay!

FARMYARD FUN

Why did the horse gallop round and round a melon?

It was a canter-loop

What should you say if you're attacked by a baby goat?

You're kidding me

FARMER ONE: *What did you call your flock of female sheep?*

FARMER TWO: Ewe herd!

How do you gather crops quickly?

Combine harvesters

I'M SERIOUSLY JOKING

Where is the milk always fresher?

On the udder side

What do you call the practice of yelling at farm animals?

Aggroculture

Why did the two farmers have an argument?

One took a fence

What do you call someone who only grows medicinal crops?

Farmer-ceutical

FARMYARD FUN

What do shepherds say when they have a drink?

Shears

What do you need to write on bacon?

A pig pen

KNOCK-KNOCK JOKES

When you first start writing knock-knock jokes it's like fishing in a trout farm. Wherever you cast your line there's a hungry fish – or funny joke – virtually leaping out at you. But the pond only contains a limited number of fish, so after a while it gets harder and harder to catch one. They're still in there, lurking around in the depths, but you need to work for your supper. Having already written several hundred knock-knock jokes, these twenty fine specimens took quite a lot of effort, but I did eventually catch them all.

I'M SERIOUSLY JOKING

Knock, knock...

Who's there?

Wide

Wide who?

Wide you ask ... can't you see who it is?

Knock, knock...

Who's there?

Dozen

Dozen who?

Dozen matter what my name is. It's a joke.

Knock, knock...

Who's there?

Garden

Garden who?

I'm garden your front door. You can't be too careful these days.

KNOCK-KNOCK JOKES

Knock, knock...

Who's there?

Spider

Spider who?

I spider hole in your fence. You might want to get it fixed.

Knock, knock...

Who's there?

Loquat

Loquat who?

I loquat you've done with your house!

I'M SERIOUSLY JOKING

Knock, knock...

Who's there?

Nautical

Nautical who?

This is nautical joke! I'll try to do better next time.

Knock, knock...

Who's there?

Tortoise

Tortoise who?

You tortoise all your best jokes.

KNOCK-KNOCK JOKES

Knock, knock...

Who's there?

Norway

Norway who?

 There's Norway I'm telling you my name!

Knock, knock...

Who's there?

Camelot

Camelot who?

I've Camelot of miles today. Let me in.

Knock, knock...

Who's there?

Picture

Picture who?

I picture rubbish up off your front lawn. It was an awful mess.

I'M SERIOUSLY JOKING

Knock, knock...

Who's there?

Holden

Holden who?

 Holden a minute ... I'm trying to think of another joke.

Knock, knock...

Who's there?

Watch

Watch who?

Watch you call me?

Knock, knock...

Who's there?

Eucalyptus

Eucalyptus who?

Eucalyptus when you were coming out of your driveway! Call your insurance company.

KNOCK-KNOCK JOKES

Knock, knock...

Who's there?

Hurdle

Hurdle who?

I've hurdle your jokes before, and they're not very funny.

Knock, knock...

Who's there?

Snot

Snot who?

Snot my greatest knock-knock joke!

Knock, knock...

Who's there?

Cedar

Cedar who?

 I cedar door, so I knocked on it.

Knock, knock...

Who's there?

Waiter

Waiter who?

Waiter minute... I think I'm at the wrong house

KNOCK-KNOCK JOKES

Knock, knock...

Who's there?

Lichen

Lichen who?

I'm lichen what you've done with your house.

Knock, knock...

Who's there?

Ivan

Ivan who?

Ivanother joke for you!

Knock, knock...

Who's there?

Weird

Weird who?

Weirdone with knock-knock jokes. Do you want an alphabet joke instead?

EASY AS ABC

The occasional alphabet joke has come to me over the years while working on different collections, such as:

Why are there only twenty-five letters in the alphabet at Christmastime?

Noel

I wasn't sure that I'd be able to squeeze twenty more out, but they came surprisingly quickly. In fact, they were as easy as A, B, C ...

I'M SERIOUSLY JOKING

Why did the alphabet lose its last letter?

It couldn't control Z

How can you tell when the alphabet has a pimple?

X marks the spot

What comes after the alphabet?

The betabet

Which is the cutest letter of the alphabet?

R!

EASY AS ABC

★ **Why is the alphabet not cool?** ★

There's a B in the AC

What car did U give to X?

A VW

Why did the sailor say 'A, B... A, B... A, B...'

He was lost at C

I'M SERIOUSLY JOKING

 What does the alphabet wear to bed?

One Z

Which letter of the alphabet takes the longest?

Q

EASY AS ABC

What comes after a lemon?
(sounds like LMN)

O

Can you say the alphabet backwards?

 It's easy ... The alphabet backwards

What did F say when it was overtaken?

G whizz

What did the boy do when he saw the alphabet in a urinal?

He took a P

I'M SERIOUSLY JOKING

I'm convinced there are only twenty-five letters in the alphabet. I don't know Y.

How do you make the alphabet lose its C?

Poke it in the i

Which part of the alphabet has the most atmosphere?

The O zone

What did the C say when it was left out of a word?

That's a K

EASY AS ABC

☆ *Why is the alphabet safe to drink?* ☆

There's NO P in it.

What happened when S whispered to T?

U heard!

When does the alphabet take a break?

It stops for T

WHO'S WHO HOWLERS

I've always enjoyed these classic name jokes, but I never imagined I'd be able to write fifty of them and still be going strong. Can you find your own name in this section? If not, email me and I'll see if I can use it in a joke. No promises, though, because I still haven't managed to turn Tom into a punchline.

What do you call a girl sitting on a slice of bread?

Marj

What do you call a boy who always runs after from you?

Chase

What do you call a boy who can't pass water?

Pierre

What do you call a girl climbing the walls?

Ivy

WHO'S WHO HOWLERS

What do you call a lady lying in a burger bun?

Patty

What do you call two men stuffed into a wallet?

Bill and Buck

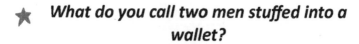

What do you call a boy sitting on a shark's back?

Finn

What do you call a guy who's no longer ill?

Manuel

What do you call a girl lying across a ravine?

Bridget

WHO'S WHO HOWLERS

What do you call a boy whose trousers are on fire?

Bernie

What do you call a girl lying in the middle of a motorway?

Elaine

 What do you call an atheist man?

Godfrey

What do you call a girl lying in a cow field?

Pat

What do you call a boy with a cat on his head?

Matt

I'M SERIOUSLY JOKING

What do you call a man who decorates your bathroom?

Tyler

What do you call a girl who's impossible to find?

Heidy

What do you call a boy who lives in a narrow valley?

Glenn

What do you call a girl hanging from a washing line?

Peggy

WHO'S WHO HOWLERS

★ *What do you call a boy who says it how* ★
it is?

Frank

What do you call a girl with sausages on
her head?

Barbie

ROMAN RIOT

After the success of my Ancient Egyptian jokes in *I'm Joking*, I thought I'd give Roman jokes a go. Perhaps because their civilisation didn't last as long as the Egyptians', it was considerably more difficult to excavate twenty Roman jokes.

I'M SERIOUSLY JOKING

Which ships did they use in the Roman Empire?

Dictatorships

How did the Romans vote?

Forum

What do you call rows of mallards across a river?

Aquaducks

ROMAN RIOT

Which combs still contain Ancient Roman hair?

Catacombs

 ### Why didn't Romans use maps?

All roads led to Rome

What did the centurion say when his troops stormed a restaurant?

Seize-a-salad

Why were most Roman roads straight?

They were designed by their rulers

What's the problem with Roman Lego?

You can't build it in a day

What do you call a monster that swallows a warrior princess?

Glad-he-ate-her

ROMAN RIOT

Why did the centurions wage battle all over the Empire?

They were roamin'

Who put the Roman candles in the Roman sandals?

Roman vandals

Where did color-blind Romans go?

The color-see-em

Why could people never figure out the population of Rome?

They never came to their census

What did the centurion say to the slave in his boat?

Row-man

I'M SERIOUSLY JOKING

Why did the pleb get beaten by a sapling?

It was the infant-tree

What did the Roman say when frozen lettuce fell from the sky?

Hail Caesar

Why did the Romans wash their hands of the Celts?

They were revolting

What ruined Roman trousers?

Their color-knees

ROMAN RIOT

☆ *Where did the Romans go for a savage haircut?* ☆

The barberians

Who refereed sporting events in Ancient Rome?

The Roman Umpire

SMARTY-PANTS JOKES

Often when
you're exchanging jokes,
someone will tell an oldie that
everyone's heard a squillion
times before. This collection gives
you alternative responses to some
of those common jokes, so you
can still get a laugh, even
when someone else is
telling the joke. You
just might look
like a bit of a
Smarty-pants!

Why did the banana go to the doctor?

~~It wasn't peeling well~~

For personal reasons. He'd rather not talk about it.

Knock, knock,

Who's there?

Boo

~~Boo who?~~

Agh! You gave me a fright!

SMARTY-PANTS JOKES

What time should you go to the dentist?

~~Tooth hurty~~

Whenever you can get an appointment

What do you get if you cross a vampire and a snowman?

~~Frostbite~~

A cold-blooded killer

What's brown and sticky?

~~A stick~~

Brown glue

What do you call a deer with no eye?

~~No eye deer~~

Visually impaired

SMARTY-PANTS JOKES

What do you do when you see a spaceman?

~~Park in it, dude~~

Call NASA

Why can't Elsa have a balloon?

~~She'll let it go~~

Because it's not her birthday

What do you call a fly with no wings?

~~A walk~~

A raisin

My dog's got no nose.

How does he smell?

~~Awful~~

I don't know... It doesn't make scents!

What's a pirate's favourite letter?

~~R~~

The one he gets from his mum every birthday!

What do you call cheese that isn't yours?

~~Nacho cheese~~

Not my cheese

 Why do seagulls live by the sea?

~~Because if they live over the bay, they'd be bagels~~

Because they eat fish

SMARTY-PANTS JOKES

★ ***How do we know that the ocean is friendly?*** ★

~~It waves~~

It rocks your boat!

How do you stop an astronaut's baby from crying?

~~You rocket~~

You give it some space

What is a tornado's favourite game?

~~Twister~~

Paper, scissors, rock!

What's worse than biting into an apple and finding a worm?

~~Biting into an apple and finding half a worm~~

World famine

SMARTY-PANTS JOKES

What is a witch's favourite subject in school?

~~Spelling~~

Dark art!

Why did the cookie go to the hospital?

~~It felt crummy~~

It got hit by a jar

 What did one plate say to the other plate?

~~Dinner is on me~~

Nothing! Plates can't talk

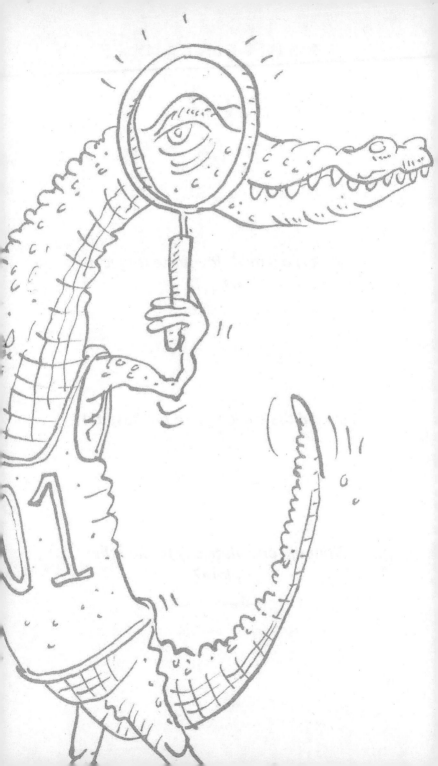

READERS' FAVOURITES

I love hearing jokes
from my readers. If you've got
an absolute favourite joke that you
love to tell, please email it to:

TomE@writelaugh.com

Remember to send me your name,
age and country, and I'll try to
include it in my next joke book.

How do you make a tissue dance?

You put a little boogie in it

Billie, age 8
Sydney, Australia

They dig, we dig, I dig, and you dig.

It's not a good poem, but it's deep.

Renee Brunt, age 11
Rotorua, New Zealand

What did the cheese say when it saw itself in the mirror?

Halloumi

Dominic, age 9
Dubai, UAE

I wrote a song about a tortilla. Actually, maybe it's more of a rap.

Jens, age 8
The Netherlands

READERS' FAVOURITES

Why did the police officer arrest the snowman?

He was up to snow good!

Dylan P, age 9
Pinner, England

Why did the chicken cross the road?

To get to the other side!

Why did the monkey cross the road?

He was stapled to the chicken!

Kallen P, age 6
Pinner, England

I'M SERIOUSLY JOKING

What do you call a Spanish man who has lost his car?

Carlos

Theo, age 9
Singapore

Why should you never argue with a ninety-degree angle?

Because they are always right!

Joe Julian, age 9
Rotorua, New Zealand

What type of maths does a butterfly do?

Mothimatics

Nitara Sablok
Auckland, New Zealand

 ## What do you call a zebra that doesn't have any stripes?

A coward

Kaysen Weston, age 7
California, USA

READERS' FAVOURITES

How did the monkey make its toasted cheese sandwich?

Under a gorilla

Oscar, age 9
Rotorua, New Zealand

I ate a clock yesterday, it was very time-consuming. Especially when I came back for seconds.

Charlie Mills, age 13
Tauranga, New Zealand

I'M SERIOUSLY JOKING

What do you call an insignificant elephant?

Irrelevant

By Bill Spilka, aged 91
Valencia, CA

Why did Tigger look down the toilet?

He was trying to find Pooh

By Zac, aged 10
Birmingham, UK

KEEP GOING

Thanks for reading I'm Seriously Joking.

Seriously.

Thank you.

If you're still hungry for more jokes, don't panic. I'm not done yet.

I write new jokes almost every day and include some of my favourites in a monthly newsletter. Go to my website www.tomemoffatt.com/keepjoking to subscribe now. I'll also let you know when I release a new joke book or hold a fun giveaway.

If you're seriously serious about jokes, turn the page to check out my other books. There are plenty more jokes, plus books that teach you how to write and tell jokes. You can even create your own favourite joke book with the Joke Collector's Notebook - a handy journal for serious jokers.

ALSO BY TOM E. MOFFATT

I'M JOKING

Still hungry for more?

Fill yourself up with *I'm Joking* - my first collection of 500+ original jokes for kids.

From barking mad dog jokes to stinky poo gags, these jokes are so fresh and funny that people will think you made them up yourself. Which is fine, as long as you remember to buy me a doughnut when you're a world-famous comedian.

THE JOKE COLLECTOR'S NOTEBOOK

Need somewhere to store your favourite jokes?

Jot them down in *The Joke Collector's Notebook*, complete with 100 illustrated jokes, fun challenges, and handy tips on finding and telling jokes.

For a FREE Word document version, go to:

www.TomEMoffatt.com/notebook

YOU'RE JOKING - VOLUME 1

BECOME AN EXPERT JOKE-TELLER

Tired of no one laughing at your jokes?

You don't have to be.

Joke-telling is a skill, like playing the piano or juggling live hedgehogs.

This book teaches you that skill using easy-to-follow instructions and simple exercises. With 101 hilarious jokes (and lots of practice), you'll soon get the laughter and applause you deserve, without ever needing to juggle hedgehogs.

YOU'RE JOKING - VOLUME 2

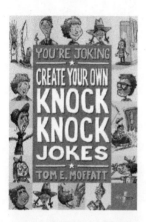

CREATE YOUR OWN KNOCK-KNOCK JOKES

Want to knock bad jokes on the head?

Learn everything there is to know about knock-knock jokes, from their history and types, to crafting your own knock-out punchlines.

Packed full of tips, prompts and 100+ hilarious examples, this book gives you the tools you need to create thousands of your own jokes. With easy-to-follow exercises (and plenty of practice!), you'll become so funny your friends will be knocking your door down for more jokes.

BONKERS SHORT STORIES

These hilarious, action-packed stories transport you to a world where mind-swapping is possible. But be warned: Looking in the mirror will never be the same again.

VOLUME 1:
MIND-SWAPPING MADNESS

A boy in a fly's body.

A toad waiting to be kissed.

Horses that know Morse code and aliens who hijack children's bodies. Has everyone gone completely bonkers?

VOLUME 2:
BODY-HOPPING HYSTERICS

Not all superpowers are a good thing.

Especially NOT if your mum has them. Or if they're fuelled by embarrassment. And what if you can't find your way back home?

ABOUT THE AUTHOR

Tom E. Moffatt was born in West London back in the twentieth century. He was such an ugly baby that his dad said, "Do we really have to take that home?"

Fortunately for Tom, they did, though due to various ailments he had to revisit the hospital so often that he was nicknamed the Reject.

Since he was young, travelling has been one of Tom's biggest passions. He spent many years backpacking and living in far-flung parts of the world, taste-testing exotic cuisines while providing a similar experience for the local mosquitoes.

These days Tom lives in Rotorua, New Zealand, with his wife and three daughters. It's hard to tell if he is still ugly because a beard covers most of his face, but he is still the butt of the occasional family joke. Instead of travelling, he spends his spare time writing jokes and stories, and loves hearing that they've been enjoyed in far-flung parts of the world.

You're still here?

Okay, maybe you could do me a favour and leave a review online? I know that it's a pain and that authors are always banging on about it. But the simple fact is ... reviews help to sell books. Potential buyers look at those reviews and if they like what other readers say, they are more likely to click *Buy*.

If you really don't fancy writing one yourself, I'll make it even easier for you. You can simply choose the most appropriate template below for any book that you read:

★★★★★ Wow. _____ was utterly brilliant. It was so good that even my cat enjoyed it.

★★★★ _____ was an absolutely incredible read, but the only book in the universe that truly deserves five stars is _____.

★★★ _____ was pretty good, but nowhere near as enjoyable as playing with my cat.

★★ _____ looks terrible. I haven't read it but am almost certain it would only deserve two stars.

★ _____ was totally awful. I am now going to eat cat food in an attempt to disguise the bad taste it has left in my soul.